Dodd, Mead Wonderland Books

The Everglades: Florida Wonderland
Greece: Wonderland of the Past and Present
Hawaii: Pacific Wonderland
Southwest Desert Wonderland
Spain: Wonderland of Contrasts

Ávila, one of the oldest cities in Castile, dates back to the Romans. The great walls still surrounding the city were rebuilt by Alfonso VI of Spain before A.D. 2000. These walls entirely enclose the old city, with eighty-eight towers, nine portals, and several smaller gateways. Ávila is set at a high elevation, surrounded on three sides by steep mountains. Winters are bitter and summers pleasantly warm. The area is popular for winter sports and seasonal trout fishing and for hunting in a nearby state game preserve, where ibex, or mountain goat, abound. The less exotic burro, pictured here, is Spain's most common animal, except for cats and dogs. Farm work and much of rural transportation would come to a standstill if the country's thousands of hard-working little beasts ever went on strike.

MAUREEN DALY

was born in County Tyrone, Northern Ireland, and grew up in Fon du Lac, Wisconsin. She first won literary distinction when she was fifteen, with a short story entitled *Fifteen*, which placed fourth in a national short story contest sponsored by *Scholastic* Magazine. The next year she won first place with a story called *Sixteen*, which was selected for the annual O. Henry Memorial Award volume. Her first novel, *Seventeenth Summer*, won the Dodd, Mead Intercollegiate Literary Fellowship contest and quickly became a best seller. She has never stopped writing since—writing vigorously, simply, and always with a new appeal.

Her articles and short stories have appeared in many national magazines. As a reporter-columnist for the *Chicago Tribune*, and, later, as an associate editor of *Ladies Home Journal* and consultant to the editors of the *Saturday Evening Post*, Miss Daly toured the United States, writing about and observing the American scene. In 1952, she was awarded the American Freedom Foundation Medal for reporting. *Mention My Name in Mombasa*, written with her husband, William P. McGivern, and her *Spanish Roundabout* are fresh, spirited reports of visits to Europe and Africa.

Seventeenth Summer is currently in preparation for movie production by Warner Brothers, and *The Ginger Horse* will be seen as a Walt Disney television presentation.

SPAIN
Wonderland of Contrasts

By Maureen Daly

ILLUSTRATED WITH PHOTOGRAPHS

DODD, MEAD & COMPANY, NEW YORK

The Jota Aragonesa *of the Aragoniana is among the favorite folk dances of the Spanish people, who love dancing so much. Here, in a country field, the castanets snap, the girl's mantilla flys in the wind and the broad silk belt of the typical native man's costume gleams in the sunlight as these two young dancers enjoy the swinging rhythm.*

FOR DOROTHY BRYAN, WITH WHOM I HAVE
SHARED SO MANY SPLENDID ADVENTURES

Thanks to Pan American World Airways and to the Spanish National Tourist Office for their generous and imaginative cooperation in supplying the splendid pictures of Spain which enliven these pages, and a special *muchas gracias* to Pan American for the magnificent photograph of the castle on this book jacket.

Contents

Olives, along with oranges and cork bark, are one of the three major exports of southern Spain. The gnarled trees, with delicate gray-green foliage, can live for many productive decades under the ideal "nine months' sun and three months' rain" climate of the south. The best grade of olive oil comes from the first pressing of the green olives. A slightly inferior quality comes from the second pressing, and the third produces an oil that is usually bitter and harsh to the taste. Much of Spanish cooking is done in olive oil, and to many low-income diets, the rich product serves as a valuable protein addition. Some olive groves are neatly aligned on fertile flatlands, other trees twist up the man-made terraces of the mountains, sending out tough roots to find nourishment in the sparse soil.

I

Spain, Land of Striking Contrasts

About three months ago, on a clear October morning, we jetted into Madrid from New York City, lowering down from 4,000 feet and circling over the flat fields of central Spain just as the morning sun touched pink on the landscape. The tawny farm lands, so often compared to the stretched hide of a great bull, seemed without motion in the early-morning light. Below us Madrid sprawled out wide, spotted green with parks and leafy boulevards, an unexpected urban oasis on the dry land.

At the airport a pretty uniformed Spanish stewardess helped us from the plane, waving a smiling *adios* with impeccably clean white gloves, all darned and frayed at the fingertips. A few wealthy Spanish passengers were met by uniformed chauffeurs and led off to shiny black cars; we drove into Madrid in the airlines bus, a lumbering old vehicle with a fare of just twenty-five cents per passenger, including luggage.

It was Sunday, and the broad highway leading into the capital city was awake with more than motor traffic. Near the outskirts of town we watched rural shepherds leading their flocks to graze in the scrubby roadside fields, now half-filled with apartment-building construction. The sheep, brown and dusty against brown dust, wandered and nuzzled among the bricks and steel beams of construction clutter, looking for grass. At a distance we sighted a man and his young son, both in boots and doeskin jackets, carrying rifles, out looking for rabbits in a suburban area that had been open field until about a year ago.

The old, sophisticated town of Madrid, seat of the government of Spain and home for more than 3,000,000 people, is slow to come awake on Sundays. Here and there cabdrivers had parked their cars—some twenty years old, but polished to a high shine—at the curb, and were dozing or looking at a Sunday pictorial paper. Doormen hosed down the sidewalks in front of elegant apartment houses, turning the spray on potted ferns and plants and shouting off an occasional country gypsy who had wandered into town to loiter and beg. Young *muchachas*, teenaged housemaids, neat in Sunday black silk uniforms, rushed along the streets to early Mass, shiny dark hair covered with small lacy mantillas.

Madrid, the capital of Spain, is a bustling, often elegant city that is bursting out its suburbs. In ten years, more than two million Spaniards have moved into this town, and in an emergency housing program, thousands of apartment housing units have been built on the fringes of Madrid. They are ultra-modern, glass-and-balconies buildings for middle-income newlyweds and larger families alike. In matters of behavior, Spaniards are usually strict self-disciplinarians and Madrileños are characteristically well groomed, formal, and citified, even on small incomes. Good shops, theaters, museums, and art galleries make this a satisfying home for sophisticated Spaniards. Here, and in other large cities, television has become popular and after an apéritif in a sidewalk café, it is pleasant to go home to a city apartment to watch an hour or two of American-produced television shows, then dinner at eleven o'clock, and off to bed.

This village street is typical of "white Spain," the sunbaked south, where narrow streets make cooling shadows and whitewashed walls are thick to keep out heat— and some of the winter chill. The balconies are used for drying clothes, raising flowers, sunning cats, and chatting across to neighbors. Most daylight hours, and until long after midnight, these streets hum with activity. But in the high-sun heat of summer, an afternoon siesta is the common custom. From around two to five o'clock, the village will be silent as a ghost town.

Over the city hung a growing hum of traffic and awaking human activity, the warm light of a Spanish sun rising above the old stone buildings, and the resonant clang of church bells—summoning bells that have rung out over Catholic Spain for centuries.

In even so short a ride—from airport to capital—we catch a glimpse of several facets of life that are typical of all Spain: side by side live the rich and the poor, the new and the old, the traditional and the progressive, and, symbolically, the awake and the asleep.

In a thousand ways this ancient, colorful country is a land of striking contrasts.

9

2

The Land Itself

Set as it is between two continents, Europe and Africa, and between two seas, the Atlantic and the Mediterranean, Spain has long been both a bridge between cultures and a mixing place for the races, ideas, and civilizations of both continents. Yet the Pyrenees Mountains have always acted as a natural northern barrier along the border of France, and the blue Mediterranean is a vast moat that separates Africa decisively from the southern shores of Spain. Close as its neighbors are, Spain seems to stand alone, neither quite European nor quite African.

Coming after Russia and France, Spain is the third largest country in Europe, and its 193,671 square miles represent about a twentieth part of all European soil.

To find a geographical feature typical of all Spain is impossible. It is an exceptionally mountainous country, both in the north and the south, with the highest mean altitude (1,950 feet above sea level) on the continent of Europe, outdistanced only by Switzerland. Its central plateau, occupying nearly two-fifths of the entire country, stretches out flat as a football field. Except for the 569 miles of the Portuguese frontier and the 281 miles of the Pyrenean isthmus, Spain is entirely surrounded by water, 1,965 miles of Atlantic and Mediterranean coast lines which are mostly high and rockbound, but with a few excellent sandy beaches.

Just as the country has great contrasts in the ups and downs of the land, so the climate has great peaks and valleys. The northern sections usually experience cool, green summers and bitingly cold winters, the flat central plateaus vary from cold in the winter to scorching heat in the summer, and the coast line areas customarily enjoy nine months of sea-cooled sunshine and three winter months of persistent gray rains.

This rice crop, under cultivation on the island of Majorca, is much like the many rice paddies that cover the middle farm lands of Spain's east coast, especially around the old port town of Valencia. At planting time, when the fields are inches deep in water, the farmer will ride behind his horse, standing on a broad, flat paddle, like a surfboard, as he sows seed in close rows. Rice is this country's chief cereal crop. Young rice plants are a high, tender green in color and this freshness, plus the blossoms on fruit trees, make a breathtaking explosion of spring beauty.

In the United States I have lived for lengths of time in Wisconsin, Pennsylvania, and California but never, even in the highest heat of California's San Fernando Valley, have I felt so trapped and stifled as in Spain's southern city of Seville in August, when the heat in the city plaza was so intense, so all-encompassing, that we sat in a parked car, windows closed, the temperature inside in the high nineties—to get

11

cool. And in the blustering, snowy winters of Wisconsin I was never so bitterly chilled as walking the streets of Spain's northern cathedral town of Burgos in late November, with winds blowing in from nearby snow-capped mountains. I remember one late morning watching children rushing home from school, with home-knit socks pulled up over their knees and home-knit stocking caps pulled down over their eyes, bucking the wind whistling through the narrow streets of the ancient town. At that moment the old cathedral bells began to ring out the noontime Angelus, and in the crisp, frosted air the noise was so acute, so clanging against my cold-stiffened face that the sound made my teeth ache. Cold and its effects never seemed that penetrating, even in northern Wisconsin.

Quite naturally the differences in topography and climate of Spain also produce a wide difference in vegetation. The south and east, blessed with the warm winds of the Mediterranean, are dotted with orange and olive groves, rice fields, palm trees, cork forests, and brilliant year-round flowers blooming in gardens and window boxes. Here the Spanish geranium, often a climbing variety, can grow tall and sturdy enough to be raised as a protective hedge around little country *fincas.*

In the north mountains are covered with thick woods of oak, chestnut, and walnut and, higher up, lofty pines, majestic trees that are often hidden from sight in swirling mountain mists. Northern valleys are bright green with good pasturelands, and the soil is excellent for vegetable farming and apple orchards.

In the northern woods squirrels, chamois, wild goats, and boar are common, but in the drier areas, except for mice, moles, and stringy, fast-legged jackrabbits, the country seems bereft of animal wild life, although it is active with domestic goat and sheep herds and pack animals such as mules and donkeys. In Africa, only a short distance over the Mediterranean from the southern port towns of Algeciras or Malaga, camels are very commonly used for transportation and as pack animals, yet I never saw a camel in Spain, except in zoos.

All Spain seems aflit with birds. Great eagles and vultures are frequent in the highest parts of the cordilleras (mountain ranges), and

12

Segovia, a town in central Spain about fifty-five miles from Madrid, is of ancient origin. It was one of the largest towns in the country in Roman times. (The population is now 30,000). The aqueduct, built by the Romans, is considered the best preserved of any that has survived. About 2,500 feet long, it is supported on 128 arches. Built of granite from the nearby Guadarrama Mountains, without the use of mortar, it carried water into Segovia until fairly recently. In the time of the Romans, the niche shown here in one of the upper columns displayed a statue of Hercules. However, the deeply religious Spanish people have long since replaced it with a statue of the Blessed Virgin Mary.

nightingales, whose song is as hauntingly sweet as fabled, warble through the warm, scented orange groves of the south. Just about five years ago flocks of white "cattle egrets," long-legged fowl that resemble miniature storks, began to migrate from Africa to southern Spain, following sheep and cattle herds to feed on animal ticks and other insects, as they did in Africa. Their white plumage and stiff, erratic walk made them stand out against the sandy shore landscape. Last summer we

13

sighted three such cattle egrets in a pasture in southern Pennsylvania, perching on the backs of cows and picking about in the grass, just as they did in Morocco and Andalusia! The species has begun the long migration to the United States.

Fishes are plentiful and widely varied all along Spain's coasts. Among the most abundant species are sardines, *merluce* (a fine white fish), anchovies, mackerel, tuna and sea bream. Frequently, for a family meal, several varieties of fried fish will be served at the same time, and for Sunday dinner a family may dine elegantly on a large *merluce*, carefully skinned, poached, and chilled, and served whole, covered with

The magnificent Castle of Coca, located about ninety miles northwest of Madrid, is a superb example of Mudejar architecture (meaning, a structure built by Moorish craftsmen in Christian times). The rose-pink structure, built in the fifteenth century, today serves as a training school for rangers and foresters. The grazing sheep and goats are as natural a part of this picture as the students themselves. Important for the products obtained from them—wool, mutton, milk, and goat cheese—these animals are accustomed to forage for any available feed. Even the lawns and shrubs of expensive homes in suburban Madrid are often nibbled at by wandering flocks, driven into town by a shepherd when summer drought dries the uncultivated grasses. At the airport in Malaga, enterprising shepherds used to turn out their flocks on the flat, grassy landing field, rounding them up three or four times a day when planes were scheduled to arrive and take off.

Tossa de Mar, a centuries-old beauty spot on the Costa Brava (Wild Coast) of northeast Spain, has been favored by travelers for hundreds of years. In fact, history unfolds in layers in this town of less than 2,000 permanent inhabitants, sitting high above a red-rocked beach, facing out to the blue Mediterranean. Phoenicians landed on these shores, ancient Romans have left traces of fortifications and the relic of a splendid villa, while the great, rough brown stone walls of Tossa were built in the twelfth century. Today, modern Spain is adding her own veneer of history, with new hotels, cafés, souvenir shops, and special off-season rates to lure artists, writers and budgeted wanderers—the twentieth-century "seaside culture" that thrives in climates with low costs and high suns. But commercial fishing boats still put out from Tossa as they did in the far-gone days of the Phoenicians.

mayonnaise. On fiesta days the mayonnaise may be artificially tinted pink or yellow. From the Mediterranean come lobster, prawns, sea bass, red mullet (a pinkish, salmon-colored fish the Spanish call "salmonete"), and *cigala*, a delicious kind of crayfish. The prawns and *cigalas* often find their way into small cafés, to be served cold with a glass of wine to customers needing a snack before Spain's traditional two-o'clock luncheon or dinner at ten in the evening.

In every town and village near enough to the sea to insure freshness, fish peddlers walk the streets in the early morning, calling out their wares to housewives who will hurry down with a platter or bowl to make a selection for lunch. Although many commercial fishing fleets, with proper refrigeration, will go out for days at a time, smaller boats frequently leave shore at three in the morning and bring in the catch at dawn. Frequently I have seen (and heard) big trucks, gears grinding, pulling out of the port town of Malaga loaded with fresh fish, hurrying up the mountain roads to Granada, to deliver the early-morning catch at the markets there. In the heat of the summer rushing the fish to market on steep roads with hairpin turns, beating the deadline of the rising, fish-spoiling sun, seemed as dramatic to me as something out of the days of the Pony Express.

Spain abounds with flowers. In the moist and fertile north, as well as in the winter-washed south, spring in Spain means an explosion of waving red field poppies, white marguerite daisies, and blue miniature iris, no more than three inches tall, spotting mountain slopes and road-side fields by the thousands. Geraniums, carnations, and calla lilies thrive in Spain, and doorways and trellises are frequently draped with blazing blankets of scarlet or purple bougainvillaea or hung with drooping wisteria vines, the cone-like clusters of flowers hanging like fragile bunches of lavender grapes. Once, on the tiny Spanish island of Ibiza, in the eastern Mediterranean, we came across a small isolated farmhouse, completely covered with huge blue morning glories. The vines had been cut away to allow the light in at the windows and door-way. The sight was so incongruous, the flowers so hid the house itself, one might easily have imagined that some chic giant had set down her flowered spring bonnet in the middle of that rocky island field.

Poinsettia bushes, a favorite in Spanish home gardens and public parks, produce dozens of big red star flowers during the winter months. In the southland scrambling jasmine bushes seem to cover every garden wall and the tiny trumpet-shaped flower, in yellow or white, smells as intensely sweet as a nightingale sounds. Young Spanish girls love to

16

This statue of the Blessed Virgin, brilliantly garbed and splendidly jeweled—but still weeping for "the children of Christ,"—is being borne on a float through the city of Seville during Holy Week. Several dozen such figures of the Virgin, each individual in appearance and ornamentation and each representing a city parish, make nightly appearances in this deeply religious parade. Many of the adornments shown here are genuine precious metals and jewels. Some belong to the parish and are kept in bank vaults between religious ceremonies. Many are lent by wealthy Sevillanas to grace the Virgin in Semana Santa. The splendor of these statues, the guttering dazzle of dozens of candles and the heady fragrance of hundreds of fresh roses, carnations, and calla lilies produce a mood of awed reverence in the watching crowds as each statue of the Virgin slowly passes by.

string jasmine blossoms into bunches to wear in their hair in the evening, and the fragrance seems to me now synonomous with dark hair and pretty faces. Surprisingly, along dry river beds or in unexpected chinks in arid mountain areas oleander bushes thrive, sometimes reaching eight and ten feet in height, blooming even under the summer sun with great pink or white clusters.

17

In large cities such as Madrid, Barcelona or San Sebastián, florist shops are as modern and elegant as one might find in New York, London, or Paris. But in the smaller towns and villages, except the most mountainous or otherwise remote, every open-air market has a flower stall or two, with great buckets of blooms waiting to be bought, along with the day's supply of fish, fruit, and bread. Unlike the Japanese, for instance, the Spanish are not devotees of flower arranging, although their gardens are frequently outstanding. But even the poorest homes seem to enjoy the "symbolic" beauty of a few flowers in the house. Four carnations, for example, may stand in the middle of a simple dinner table where the main and only course is fish soup, or grace the niche holding the statue of the Blessed Virgin, over the family sewing machine, in a crowded cottage. A Spanish housewife, considering all the needs of her family, will place flowers next in importance only after a loaf of bread.

Rainfall and flowing rivers are abundant in the north and much of the coastal areas of Spain. But in the central plains and more southerly sections, the land must be irrigated to produce. Most of the irrigation systems, networks of deep furrows of earth that can be opened or blocked off to regulate water flow, date back seven hundred years and were originated in Spain by the invading Arabs. Thus, rather than experiencing gentle or frequent rains, the southern crops—tomatoes, peppers, potatoes, melons, lettuce, and others—are given two "big drinks" a day by the tending field hands.

Looking at the whole of Spain with an eagle's-eye view, one could judge from the man-made topography that the structures needed for mining and industry are almost all concentrated in the north of the country. The rest of Spain is devoted chiefly to farming and fishing. About 40 per cent of Spain's 33,000,000 people live in cities. Two of these cities, Madrid and Barcelona, have about 3,000,000 and 1,750,000 residents respectively, and twenty-two other towns, scattered around the country, have over 100,000 inhabitants each.

But 60 per cent of all Spaniards live in the country, either in the hundreds of small villages scattered through the plains and mountains

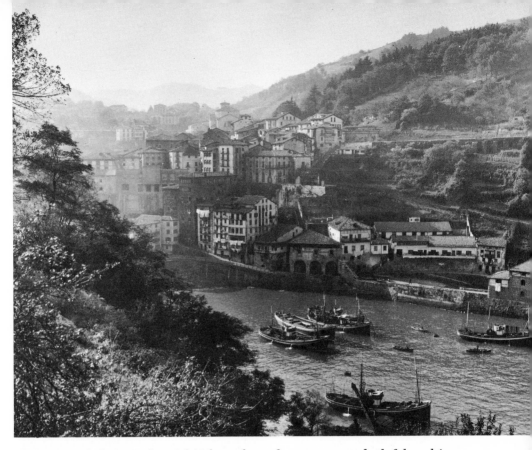

With its sturdy houses, plentiful fuel supply, and easy access to both fish and farm products, life in this northern Basque coastal town is probably just as snug as it looks. Basques are famous not only for their enormous appetites but also for their excellent and distinctive cooking. Salt cod (bacalao) dishes are a specialty of this region. One excellent dish is made by soaking the cod overnight, boning it, arranging it in layers in a casserole with sliced raw potatoes, covering this with a sauce of tomatoes, onions, and peppers, and baking. Curiously, in a trade agreement with far-off Iceland, Spain imports enormous quantities of salt cod from that island, and Iceland purchases Spanish wines in return. Recipes, somehow, have also been exchanged and one cold day in Reykjavik, Iceland's capital, I enjoyed a very authentic and delicious Basque bacalao casserole.

or in isolated farmhouses. Most of the articles manufactured in Spain are sold and used right in that country. It is the agricultural products— wines, fruits, olives, olive oil, cork—that are Spain's chief exports. Thus, this is chiefly an agricultural country, a land of plodding burros and laboring farmers, plus a number of ancient but urbane cities, with museums and universities, citizens and social customs that rank with the most sophisticated in all Europe.

19

3

From Altamira to the United Nations...

The long history of Spain is, quite naturally, so filled with names, dates, battles, conquests, and defeats that only a short listing is possible here. A few of the major events and dates in the great timetable of Spanish history will, however, highlight the vivid picture of present-day Spain.

10,000 B.C.—ROCK PAINTING: Drawings discovered on the rock walls of the hidden caves of Altamira, outside the north coastal town of Santander, show that primitive man lived here—and expressed himself artistically—in prehistoric times. Wall drawings show bison, horses, and deer.

1100 B.C.—FOUNDATION OF CÁDIZ: Still a busy, prosperous Atlantic seaport, Cádiz was founded as a Phoenician colony, later taken over by Greeks, then Romans.

113 B.C.—ROMAN COLONIZATION: Rome began an active conquest of Spain. Roman ruins of aqueducts, bridges, amphitheaters, and roads still exist as proof of the success of their conquest.

A.D. 61–67—CHRISTIANIZATION OF SPAIN BEGINS: Tradition says that St. James was the first evangelist to visit Spain; it is highly probable that St. Paul journeyed to Spain later. Catholicism is the official religion of Spain today.

A.D. 711—MOSLEM INVASION: Attacking through Gibraltar, Moorish invaders from Africa pushed up from the south of Spain, finally taking over the entire peninsula, except for mountain areas in the north. The Moors left their mark in Spain in its architecture, farming methods, social customs—and in the physical appearance and temperament of the Spaniards. Moorish domination lasted until 1492.

In Spain, there are some 1,420 castles, ranging from those regal households built by the Christians to the picturesque, crumbling fortress castles, many built by the Moslems, that dot the high shore lines of the Mediterranean Sea. Generally speaking, the Christian castle has round towers and looks like a ship moored on land or hilltop. The Moslem castles have square turrets and the high-walled, windowless look of a fortified oasis. Since 1940, the Spanish Government has directed that no castle may be altered or demolished, but many already show the ruthlessly creative touches of wind, sun, and time, with lichen and small bushes growing from crumbled walls and sheep grazing happily in roofless old halls. The castle pictured here is Marchanilla Castillo, outside Seville. Very likely the prickly paddle cactus and bright red poppies that sprinkle the meadow are blooming just as luxuriantly inside as outside the old walls.

1492—Conquest of granada: Under the Catholic Sovereigns, Ferdinand and Isabella, the Moors were driven from their last stronghold, the southern city of Granada. Spain was united as one of the strongest states in western Europe.

Discovery of america: Sponsored and financed by Ferdinand and Isabella, Christopher Columbus sailed from the Spanish port of Palos to discover America.

1509—Conquest of oran: Spanish forces made conquests in Africa. The following year, successful conquests were made at Tripoli and Algiers.

1522—First circumnavigation of the globe: Commanded first by Magellan, and after his death by Elcano, five ships set out from Sanlúcar, in Andalusia. Sailing steadily westward for three years, under extreme hardship conditions, one ship, the *Victoria*, finally arrived back at Sanlúcar, giving first experimental proof that the world is round.

This sturdy village, with its wooden houses, spired church, deep green fields, and snow-crested mountains, might well be a hamlet in Switzerland. But it is the valley village of Salardu, in the province of Lerida, in Spain's Catalonian northwest. The Pyrenees Mountains border, and then France, lie to the north. Some miles to the east is the Mediterranean Sea and the sophisticated, bustling port town of Barcelona. These lush valley fields, productive and prosperous, supply much of the agricultural products needed to feed the industrial coastal towns. The area can be bitter cold in winter, blasted by snow-chilled mountain winds and shaded from the sun by high peaks. Then farmers don heavy sheepskin coats and high leather gaiters and even the work oxen are given bulky head coverings of sheepskin or heavy wool, trimmed with swinging red tassels.

The Fiesta de San Fermin, a week-long bullfighting festival, is held annually in the city of Pamplona, high in Spain's northern Basque country. For several centuries, this fiesta has started each year at sunrise on the seventh of July. That morning, and on following mornings, to make "seven days running," seven fighting bulls are released on signal from pens behind the town hall, to gallop through a long path of barricaded streets into the bull ring. Running before the swift bulls as they bolt down the streets, slashing right and left with their horns, is considered by young Spaniards the ultimate in bravery. It does take enormous courage. One bright July sunrise I saw a boy slumped in the barred doorway of a Pamplona haberdashery, two gore wounds in his back. He had been brave—but not quite fast enough!

HERNAN CORTES CONQUERED NEW SPAIN (MEXICO): Cortes conquered the Aztec territories of Mexico for the Spanish Crown. Charles I was emperor of both the Old Continent and the New.

1535—CONQUEST OF PERU BY PIZARRO: The city of Lima was founded. In this great conquistador period, the following exploits and discoveries were accomplished in the name of Spain: 1512, Florida (Ponce de León); 1513, discovery of the Pacific (Balboa); 1536, foundation of Buenos Aires and Texas; 1540, discovery of the Grand Canyon of Colorado (Coronado); Orellana traveled down the Amazon from the Andes to the Atlantic.

1571—Battle of lepanto: Naval victory of the Holy League (Spain, Papacy, and Venice) against the Turks in the Mediterranean.

1588—Defeat of the spanish armada: Routing of the fleet sent against England by Philip II. Major disaster to the strength of the Spanish empire.

1704—Loss of gibraltar: After the death of Charles II of Spain, without issue, war spread all over Western Europe. In the subsequent fighting, an English fleet attacked and captured the Rock of Gibraltar, on Spain's south coast. Today, the British flag still flies there.

1810–1824—Emancipation of spanish america: The former Spanish Indies became independent nations from the Rio Grande to Tierra del Fuego. Out of a vast overseas empire, only Cuba, Puerto Rico, and the Philippines remained Spanish possessions.

1898—Loss of cuba, puerto rico, and the philippines: The United States intervened in Cuba's war with Spain. All three possessions were lost after heroic fighting.

1914—First world war: During this conflict, Spain remained neutral, beset by strikes and political confusion within the nation.

1936—The spanish civil war: In one of the bitterest, bloodiest civil wars of modern times, Spain battled within herself for three years. The death, destruction, and disruption of the unity of the people scarred Spain for another two decades. On April 1, 1939, the Spanish civil war ended and Generalissimo Francisco Franco became head of the government, a post he still holds today.

1939—Second world war: During this war (1939–1945) Spain again remained neutral. Her own enormous political and economic problems continued side by side with the devastation of the rest of Europe.

1965—Today: Today, Spain is a changing, prospering country, once more part of the community of Europe. Although Spain is not a member of NATO, American-Spanish naval and airbases have existed on Spanish soil since 1953, by special treaty. In 1955, Spain was admitted to the United Nations without a single dissenting vote. The country is now hopeful of joining Europe's Common Market Plan for greater economic growth and stability. All over Spain today, the government has posted signs and billboards reading: Twenty-five Years of Peace.

This eighth-century Arab mosque, in the heart of the bustling southern city of Córdoba, is one of the outstanding (and carefully preserved) architectural relics in Spain. Part of the building, which covers an area almost as large as St. Peter's in Rome, is now a Christian church. The forest of 850 jasper columns (jasper is an uncrystalline quartz) and the double Moorish arches in red and white stone stand as stunningly serene and pacifying as they did when the Moorish builders planned this structure more than one thousand years ago. It is surrounded by the Courtyard of the Orange Trees, a fragrant garden planted with the same rhythmic serenity and repetition that give this mosque its distinction. I remember visiting the place on a hot summer day, when the area was crowded inside and out, and yet the old mosque and its orange tree guardians produced a mood that seemed to equal individual silence. It was as if the building itself were at prayer.

After a turbulent and often disrupting history, the country is determined to maintain peace—with prosperity. Even though time has healed many of the deep wounds of the civil war, not all Spaniards are content under the tight, authoritarian rule of General Franco's government, yet all are now hopeful for peaceful solutions.

25

4

Buenos Días, Señoras y Señores

What does a modern Spaniard *look* like? Consider the fact that over the centuries the peninsula of Spain was invaded (or "discovered") by Phoenicians, Carthaginians, Greeks, and Romans. In the fourth and fifth centuries, Germanic barbarians swept down from the north. In the eighth century, thousands of Moors swept up from Africa—and stayed on Spanish soil for nearly eight hundred years. Thus the physical characteristics of several widely different races have melded over the years into what is today's Spaniard.

Generally speaking, Spaniards are an unusually handsome people, moderate in height, slight in build but muscular, with dark hair, dark eyes, and skin tones ranging from fair to olive. Bright eyes and lustrous hair seem characteristic (many Spaniards, as do Italians, feel their abundant and healthy hair comes from olive oil in the daily diet). As a group, they are blessed with fine, smooth skins. Even adolescents never seem plagued with the complexion problems that affect so many American teenagers, as well as young people of the northern countries of Europe.

Quite naturally, all Spaniards are not handsome or beautiful. Prosperous businessmen tend to become rotund after forty, and their wives are usually equally chubby. Harsh winds and the rugged living of tiny sea or mountain hamlets can turn the finest skin into a maze of wrinkles by the time a man is thirty-five. And poverty and poor dental work can make even a young woman an early-age crone. But I have the feeling that at *some time* in every Spaniard's life he or she is beautiful to look at.

Spanish children are often extraordinarily pretty and they are usually pampered, petted, and given the best in the house. Even the poorest

26

This imposing wooden retable ("retable" simply means shelf or ledge behind an altar) is the intricately carved, centuries-old masterpiece in Toledo. Begun in the thirteenth century and completed two hundred years later, this cathedral is filled with a tremendous number of treasures, testifying to both the piety and the indefatigability of the early Spanish Christians. There are five naves, twenty-two chapels, numerous mellow rose-glass windows, and 750 other windows. There are jeweled chalices, historic tapestries of great value, ancient church vestments, and pictures by El Greco, Velázquez, Goya, Titian, Murillo, and other superb Spanish artists. In the vast coolness and silence of Toledo's cathedral, away from the turmoil and blazing sun of the city streets, one is impressed by the sheer mass of this extraordinary religious tribute—then deeply moved by the inspired beauty of each individual masterpiece.

little village child is usually put into a clean, wash-worn smock each morning and sent out to play with a kiss. In the big cities, on Sunday afternoons, parents proudly parade their whole families on casual strolls through the parks and boulevards—small boys clad in short flannel pants and jerseys, little girls in neat coats and hats, or short dresses, smocked and pleated. Spanish women have a fine sense of chic (much like the French) and since, if they don't sew themselves, good seamstresses are cheap, most Spaniards dress very well.

Even in the villages, poor old women in black dresses and black shawls, iron-gray hair pulled into a bun, have an air of being neatly put

In the third or fourth week of April (depending on the end of the Lenten season), the exquisite old southern city of Seville bursts forth in a three-day spring feria. Drawing thousands of tourists and visitors from all over Spain, the fair is held in the Prado of San Sebastian, a wide, grassy area behind the Tobacco Factory. Four long blocks of casetas, or highly decorated tents, some with several rooms, are rented to out-of-town families, who hold three-day open house for visitors, with music, dancing, and sherry for everyone. Two main streets are cut off to auto traffic for the feria and the constant parade of mounted men in Andalusian costume and their pretty girls are part of the traditional scene. There is also a livestock show that draws breeders and the finest animals from all around the country, but it is colorful, romantic, musical, and elegantly raucous mood that is the trademark of this annual spring outburst.

This vast Roman-built amphitheater, excavated after centuries under Spanish soil, was built in 18 B.C., in the town of Mérida, near the Portuguese border. Once one of the most important cities in the Roman-Spanish world, present-day Mérida also boasts the imposing remains of a Roman circus that could hold 20,000 spectators, with gladiators' dressing rooms and pens for wild beasts still somewhat intact. The theater shown here was constructed to seat 5,500 persons; the great stage, with Corinthian pillars, was once adorned by statues, most of which have now been removed to museums. The original marble paving still floors the amphitheater. The biggest collection of Roman works in all Spain is in this town, now shrunk to a provincial 25,000 inhabitants.

together. A Spanish maid or housewife would never go to market without a fresh face, fresh dress and a touch of cologne behind the ears. Partly because the traditional *siesta* hours in the afternoon break up the day, every Spaniard looks refreshed and groomed in the late-afternoon and evening hours. Good grooming is a part of the Spanish way of life. Spaniards are full of compliments and appreciation for one another and set great value on personal good looks.

The Spaniards are also a very clean people. Often a village housewife can do more with a bucket of cold water and a handful of esparto grass (for scouring) than her American equivalent might do with a collection of electrical appliances. Quite naturally, extreme poverty, illness, or general discouragement can cause any household to become run-down, but most Spanish homes are like little "personality factories," with the mother as the foreman, intensely proud and hard-working in turning out attractive products. It is not customary for Spanish women to work outside the home after marriage (although some do), so enormous energies and strong maternal instincts are concentrated on husband and children.

The family is a very potent unit in Spain. Since there is no legal divorce, marriage must be regarded as a lifetime arrangement, and this tends to give an extra pride and stability to most homes. Since Spain is a Catholic nation, large families are the tradition, and most young marrieds look forward to having a half dozen or more children. (I had tea in Madrid one afternoon not long ago with a shiny-eyed señorita who is to be married this spring. She and her future husband had been apartment hunting. They wanted an apartment with three bedrooms—to start. One bedroom for the couple, and two bedrooms to be shared by future children. "With three bedrooms we know we will not have to move for at least four years," Maria explained. The young couple fully expected, and hoped, to have a child the first year, another the next, and so on.)

Because marriages are contracted in a serious, religious mood, and because the whole idea of the responsibilities of marriage and raising a family is so deeply instilled in the Spanish mind, teenaged marriages in that country are quite unheard of. A boy or girl may become *novio* and *novia* while in their teens but that simply means a long and carefully chaperoned engagement. Few Spanish girls marry before they are twenty-two; young men are usually a few years older. Selecting a *novio* is not at all like the American custom of "going steady." It is an announcement of a serious intention to marry and, although the arrangement may be broken, like any engagement, a girl who has more than two or three *novios* in her lifetime would be considered flighty or not respectable. During the engagement period, *novios* and *novias* may go to *fiestas* together, or for long *paseos* (ambling walks for chatting, meeting friends, perhaps stopping at a café for a *limonada*) in the evening, but most of the activities are still close to home. Dating as we know it in the United States, our custom of teenagers going out together, frequently and away from home, is almost unknown in Spain.

The Court of the Lions in the Alhambra is an excellent example of the superb workmanship of the Moorish artisans who built this palace centuries ago. The courtyard is rectangular, surrounded by a gallery supported by 124 slender white marble columns, and the passageway is paved in white marble. Its fountain is supported by twelve carved lions, highly individual, each spouting water from his mouth. The cornices over the arches are heavily worked in an airy, open design and the passage walls are tiled with colorful, precise mosaic. Today, every part of the Alhambra, from white marble to velvet-green grass and fragrant orange trees, is kept immaculately groomed, almost as if some demanding, imperious sultan still held rule. Under the spotlight of the hot Andalusian sun, this ancient palace gleams as a bit of graceful history, tantalizingly near perfection.

In considering the home life of this country, it is interesting to note that there is next to no juvenile delinquency in Spain. In spite of the fact that the Spaniards were known to act with unusual violence and passion in their own civil war, they seem unable to understand "delinquency" in ordinary life. Spanish newspapers frequently carry stories of juvenile-delinquency problems in the United States and they are considered phenomena alien to anything in the Spanish character. A friend in Malega once asked me about an article he had read of vandalism and stealing in a Connecticut high school. He was completely puzzled by the behavior. "A *gypsy* might steal," he said, "but not a *Spaniard.*"

31

Spaniards also have a great respect and courtesy, deeply instilled, for women. It is a very common practice for men to murmur *piropos,* or pretty compliments, on the public street to women—passing comments like "how beautiful!" or "such loveliness." These remarks are made, however, as compliments—lightly, quickly, and flatteringly. They are meant to praise but never to bother or worry. Because of this respect and courtesy, one is impressed with the safeness of Spanish streets and pathways for women, even after dark.

As two brief illustrations: one night I was walking home alone to a villa we had rented outside a southern village. It was late. I had taken a short cut on a back road and, in the intense darkness, I heard the sound of a donkey's hoofs approaching. My own footsteps must have sounded on the dusty road, too, for ahead of me a voice called out, "*Buenos noches, Señora*" ("Good evening, Madam"). A few moments later, a man riding the donkey passed me and said softly, "*Vaya con Dios*" ("Go with God"). It was a farmer coming home late from the fields and, with great instinctive courtesy, he had realized I might be frightened. As a second personal example, I walked back to my hotel from a late dinner party in Madrid recently. The soup course had been served promptly at 11 P.M. and it was at least half-past one in the morning when I began the stroll of a few blocks through the city streets. On the way, several men passed me. No one stopped. No one spoke. There are no *piropos* after dark. That might prove frightening, and hence discourteous.

So much that is admirable in Spanish behavior can be traced to personal pride, the deep-seated conviction within each man that he is important. This pride shows itself in many ways: the excellent good manners, ability to do small jobs well, quick wit, active personal lives, and a general zest for living. There is little that is slovenly in the Spanish character. Spaniards are strict self-disciplinarians and demand a good deal of themselves in terms of behavior. One of the most scathing comments any Spaniard might make about another is to say: "He is *sin verguenza* (without shame)."

The country of Spain is divided into fifty-four provinces—as the United States is divided—and sixteen main regions, such as Andalusia in the

El Escorial, about an hour's drive out of Madrid, is famous as a summer resort for commuting Madrilenos and as the burial place of many of the kings of Spain, from Charles I to Alfonso XII, and one queen, Isabella II. The enormous flood-lit structure shown here is the monastery of El Escorial, begun by Philip II in 1554. It was built in thanksgiving for Spanish victory in battle and designed in a gridiron shape to honor St. Lawrence, a favorite saint of the king's. ("Gridiron," in this case, does not mean football field. St. Lawrence suffered martyrdom by fire.) El Escorial, which took years to complete, has 13 chapels, 15 cloisters, 86 staircases, 1,200 doors, and 2,673 windows, plus a handsome collection of paintings and the many royal mausoleums. The little village of El Escorial, shady with mountain oaks, devotes itself almost entirely to resort and tourist business and guarding over its dead kings.

south, northern Catalonia, western Estremadura, and so forth. And there are certain differences in character that seem to identify with the different regions. For instance, it is said—by the Spaniards—that the Catalonian is thrifty, the Galician is always homesick away from home, the Andalusian sings, the Basque acts, the Estremaduran is a fighter, and the Castilian is a dreamer. The north, with its sterner climate and rough terrain, seems to produce a more rugged approach to living; the sunny south, a more lighthearted attitude. It has been said that "if the Basques bring to the Spanish character more power than grace, the Andalusians bring more grace than power."

33

5

How Do They Live...What Do They Eat?

Chill mountain valleys and low sun-baked plains; primitive fishing villages hugging the Mediterranean; or the ancient, sophisticated city of Barcelona, rising above its bustling seaport . . . with all its highly varied climate and landscape, Spain naturally has many very different types of dwellings. Local weather, available building materials and the special uses to which the houses are put all make differences.

For instance, in the north, a home must protect against snow and rain, building stone and wood are plentiful, and the farmer is likely to own his own cattle. Hence he will have a stout house of stone and wood, with a slate roof, steeply pitched in the mountain areas to cast off rain and to ease the burden of heavy snows. Such a house will likely be of two stories, with the lower floor used for livestock and the upper floor containing the kitchen and bedroom and perhaps a parlor, or *sala de respeto*, for special family occasions. A typical sight in northern Galicia and Asturias is a food larder on stilts, to protect the food inside from damp earth and rodents. This slate-roofed *horreo*, set on four high legs, is made of wood and may be completely surrounded by a catwalk or passage. Grains and pork products are stored here.

In the central plains, where the dry climate has annual extremes of both heat and cold, houses are usually one-story structures, built with the only available materials, clay and straw. Sheep and goats are the only livestock, other than burros. These houses are the same clayey color as the surrounding landscape and have few and narrow windows, in order to keep out both the brilliant light of summer and the chills of winter. Because the problem of water supply is acute here, most farmhouses are grouped together in scattered villages, and many are attached buildings, facing out on a common street. A typical feature of a

34

Cádiz, an energetic Atlantic port town of about 95,000, has long been dubbed in Spanish "the little silver cup," because of the brightness of the sea light, the gleam of white houses, and the strange, pearly sheen of miles of salt flats that line the roads into town. Fishing fleets, as pictured here, bring in catches of tuna, sardines, and other fishes to add to both the prosperity and culinary distinction of this city. In-town squares are lined with towering palm trees and fig and orange groves, grilled windows spill out with flowers, and the whole look of the town is sunlit, southern, and African. In the oldest section (Cádiz dates back over one thousand years to the Phoenicians), some streets are so narrow that neighbors can reach across, balcony to balcony, and touch hands.

La Mancha farmhouse is the rear farmyard, onto which stable and dwelling open and where the farm implements are kept. Wine cellars, in this wine-producing area, are often underground storerooms, capped by small, man-made hills.

In some parts of the plateau area, the winter heating problem is solved by means of a *gloria* or central hearth, from which run conduits to bring the heat to other rooms. The walls of these clay-and-straw houses are made very thick, to keep out summer heat and winter cold.

In southern Andalusia, on the farms or in the villages, houses of whitewashed clay brick, with cool stone floors, narrow windows with iron grillwork, and small balconies on the upper floors are most frequent. Here the patio or inner courtyard with a small fountain and potted flowers is typical.

35

Almost throughout Spain, kitchens are extremely simple, with cold running water and a charcoal stove for cooking. Refrigerators are becoming more common with the wealthy, but most households market by the day, using only fresh food products. Thousands of Spanish households still have no running water at all, and large clay jugs must be filled several times daily at the village fountain. Washing machines are still not common, and in apartments laundry work is done at a special sink in the kitchen, with built-in scrub boards, while many private homes have a little laundry house in the garden or patio. Most small

Located about 650 miles out into the Atlantic Ocean from the southernmost Spanish port town of Cádiz, but only 72 miles from the northwest coast of Africa, the seven islands of the Canaries have been Spanish ruled since late in the fifteenth century. One of the larger islands, Tenerife, shown here, is as extraordinarily beautiful, with its peaked mountains and lush hillsides, as this picture suggests. Both Christopher Columbus and Cortes, on trips to the New World, are said to have stopped to hear Mass on these historic islands while waiting to have their ships' water kegs refilled. For all their scenic beauty, the Canary Islands have an irregular economy, and often picturesque beauty barely masks the poverty of shacks on tiny farms with too-rocky soil. Besides drawing tourists from all over the world, the Canaries are important for the export of bananas—the delicate, small brown-skinned kind—and delicious, thin-skinned tomatoes, barely bigger than golf balls, that brighten many a winter table in the British Isles and northern Europe.

This slim, elegant bell tower, the Giralda, was built as the minaret of a Moorish mosque in the twelfth century. Its ancient brick, pierced by arched windows in the Arabic style, has been carefully preserved, and it stands today as the bell tower for the cathedral of Seville, the largest and most beautiful in Spain. Every day, 500 masses are said in the 80 chapels of this vast church. Christopher Columbus is buried here, in an ornate mausoleum, after having been shifted from graves in San Domingo and Havana. Seville is a graceful city whose business and home life seem to flow smoothly in and around its many superb shrines of the past. Sidewalk cafés line the streets near the great cathedral and at sundown chimes from the bell tower seem to meld with the scent of flowers in window boxes and the lace of iron balconies to create a mood uniquely Seville.

villages have a "municipal washhouse," a large, roofed shed with stone sinks and cold running water for scrubbing the family laundry.

Of all the electrical equipment common to American households, the two most frequently found in Spanish homes are the radio and electric iron. Spaniards, in crowded cities or rural villages, seem to have a greater tolerance for noise than many other people, and radios blare constantly.

In the south, where fuel is extremely scarce, most homes have no wintertime heat at all, although wealthy homes may have a fireplace in the main salon or master bedroom. Brass *braseros*, low, shallow metal containers, heaped with glowing charcoal or olive pits, are frequently set under the family dining table during the cold months, and the table is draped with a heavy cloth that touches the floor. Thus feet and legs are kept warm during the dining hours, at least. During the day, a housewife may do her sewing at that table. In the evening hours, children bring their school lessons or games there, to enjoy the small glow of heat.

Millions of Spaniards are, of course, city apartment dwellers. The wealthy live in continental elegance, with excellent paintings, furniture, silver, and crystal—and a staff of little maids to keep everything shiny. (Since a good live-in cook earns about $28.00 a month, a housemaid only $25.00, many families have two or more in help.) Most apartments, however, are simple dwellings, sparsely furnished and potentially uncomfortable, except for the great warmth of life that makes them *homes*.

In recent years, the Spanish Government has been active in planning and subsidizing building projects to improve housing conditions in all income groups. The housing, particularly because of the painful years during and after Spain's civil war, had simply become too old, too run-down, and too crowded to make people comfortable. In Madrid, as in numbers of other major cities, whole new "apartment villages" have been built for self-supporting, middle-income families, each group of big, sunny, well-planned buildings circling a large *plaza* with cafés, open-faced food stalls for shopping and *perfumerias* and beauty shops so essential to the Spanish housewife.

Over the past decade, at government urging, thousands of Spanish workers have migrated from the south to find employment, in the more prosperous north. Dreadful migrant shack towns, with deplorable living conditions, had begun to grow up around the major cities. In a special building program (the Ministry of Housing hopes to have built 4,000,000 new dwellings by 1975), the "instant slums" were bulldozed down and their inhabitants transferred to numbers of new, clean, and

These southern gypsies, colorfully costumed and carefully posed, are ready to go into a wild flamenco dance at the click of a castanet or the drop of a tourist tip. Droves of these unusual people live in cave homes cut out of the chalky rock of the Sacromonte Grotto, outside Granada. The caves are often ornately furnished with rugs, brass lamps, and tapestry wall hangings. Few gypsy children ever go to school. It is more profitable to join their parents in entertaining tourists or performing in little Spanish night clubs. Less colorful, but more personally appealing, are the scores of "river gypsies," eternal transients who rove up and down the southern roadways, walking in families or driving shabby wagons, camping at any chance stream of water, and weaving baskets to sell in town for food. Many gypsies, proud of their skill in begging, traverse regular weekly routes, accosting businessmen or knocking at specific household doors with the regularity of traveling salesmen. Once I went to England for a month. When I returned to our home outside Malaga, "my gypsy" informed me I was four weeks behind in contributions.

efficient suburban villages. To date, the program has been so successful that architects have traveled to Spain from as far away as Australia and South America to study the villages.

I spent some time visiting the six separate "villages" built on the outskirts of Madrid. These were simple but well-planned little towns, circling a plaza with a small modern church. These villages are like modern versions of the pueblos of the Southwest in the United States. (Three of the little towns had the odd names of The Grape, Holy Bread, and Uncle Raymond's Well!)

Rental of a small house here, with indoor bathroom and running water, is about $4.00 a month, occupancy limited to families with a joint income of $100 a month or less. In many of the new villages, families may arrange to buy the homes, rather than rent. As part of the program, "model houses" are fitted out with simple but sturdy and well-designed furniture, plus everything a beginning household might need, from pots and pans to lamps. At a very low payment per month, householders may completely furnish a new home to suit their needs. In some parts of the southern countryside, run-down and impoverished villages have been replaced in the same way—with new church, school, market place, streets, and all.

Knowing the strong individualism of the Spaniard, I asked my escort, a representative of the Ministry of Housing, if the people had objected to moving out of their slum homes into the new villages. He answered tersely, "Of course not. No man prefers to live in filth."

In housing, as in most phases of life, contrasts between the rich and the poor are striking. In Seville or Malaga, for instance, the great, many-roomed private homes, surrounded by vast, blooming gardens, hemmed in by high iron fences, or the sprawling ranch houses of the bull farms

For centuries, this ancient castle outside the little Castilian town of Penafiel has dominated its hilltop lookout, watching over an impressive parade of history. Nearby, in the important old town of Valladolid, the Catholic kings, Ferdinand and Isabella, were married in 1469. A quarter of a century later, a bitter, weary Christopher Columbus journeyed back to Valladolid to die. At the beginning of the 1800's, Napoleon himself was quartered in the old town. Valladolid is still famous for its university and fine old museums, but its gardens and courtyards are no longer the meeting places of kings. The once-proud castle plays host to students and tourists and an occasional shepherd who pauses to eat his bread and cheese in the shadow of its turrets.

Toledo, about forty-five miles from Madrid, is often called "the museum city" because it has over thirty major historical sights to see, plus the picturesque daily excitement of life in a jammed and jumbled old town that has been a focal point of art and metal crafts for centuries. After a sight-seeing tour over rough cobbled streets to visit El Greco's home, the Museum of San Vincente, with a vast collection of his fine paintings, the busy Plaza de Zocodover (meaning in Spanish and Arabic "A Market to See") and the famous Alcazar fort, scene of heroic fighting in the Spanish Civil War, the flat waters of the Tagus and cool shadows of the Bridge of San Martin make a soothing resting place. I remember that once a To-ledo policeman routed us out of a local park during siesta *time (one is supposed to rest in hotels or at home), so we found a sheltered rock near the river and watched storks circle the bridge towers while Toledo napped.*

or large *fincas* are in sharp contrast to the limited comfort of the "new" villages. In Spain, the rich live very rich, indeed.

Even with extensive new building, no part of Spain is ever far from the historical *old*. In every town, in every part of the countryside, remnants of past centuries and glories exist side by side with the structures of modern life. History is everywhere. In Segovia, a huge stone aqueduct, built by the Romans centuries ago, runs through the heart of town. In Seville, bells ring out for Mass from an exquisite bell tower built to call the Moors to Moslem services in the twelfth century. In Barcelona, everyday life in the little streets of the old section are overshadowed by the historic cathedral, dedicated to Santa Eulalia, which took more than three centuries to build. In every sunlit old street, in every shadowed cathedral, the Spaniards of the past seem to live side by side with the Spaniards of today.

41

6

That Smells Good...What Is It?

The food that finds its way to a family dinner table can often tell much about a country and the people in it—climate, terrain, fertility of soil, average income, and tastes of the people, plus the "civilization" of their cooking skills.

Spanish foods—and Spanish cooking—are rich in variety. Yet the most popular dishes are not highly spiced nor made hot with dried peppers, as is so much Mexican food. Spanish cooking is more nearly comparable to the fine, blending skills for which the French are so famous.

Although systems for food transportation are improving, small villages and isolated hamlets must often make do with what grows in their own fields or what roams on their own pastures, but here are some of the varieties of food commonly available to the Spanish kitchen: rice and wheat products; sheep, pigs, and beef cattle in the north; a wide variety of fish, olive oil for cooking; a range of vegetables from cabbages, potatoes, and turnips to plentiful supplies of green peppers, onions, zucchini, tomatoes, and artichokes; fruits such as oranges, lemons, and grapefruit, apples, figs, pomegranates, melons, and grapes (Spain has many avocado trees but few seem to enjoy this rich salad fruit). Besides all this, there are eggs and poultry (new methods of chicken farming are producing plumper chickens), milk, and a variety of cheeses, mostly of the hard, dry kind and not nearly so good as French or Italian cheeses.

It is said that when Napoleon and his troops were stationed in Spain, many decades ago, they valued Spanish recipes enough to bring them back to French chefs. Certainly, various regions of Spain have produced certain foods and recipes that are worth remembering and reproducing.

In the bull ring of Pamplona, this matador is saluting the crowd after having circled the ring in a triumphal trot. Once, in this bull ring, we saw popular Jaime Ostos, standing at the barrera, *dedicating his bull to some young lady before his* corrida *began. Through horrifying mismanagement, the bull was let into the ring at that moment. The animal sighted the little gold-suited figure, far across the sand, standing with arms raised, back to the bull. The animal charged and Ostos mistook the warning screams of the crowd as shouts of enthusiasm. The giant bull butted the matador squarely in the back, miraculously without goring him, and tossed him into the crowd like a limp doll. The next afternoon, Jaime Ostos was back to fight the bulls, pale but courageous, with nothing more than two Band-aids on his handsome face.*

In Estremadura, where acorns are plentiful, the pig herds are well fed and the area produces excellent ham and sausage. A certain kind of Spanish ham, *serrano*, is cured in the cold of mountain snows, and it is nutty in flavor, dark red in color, and almost translucent when sliced.

From Andalusia comes *gazpacho*, a cold soup now served quite often in American restaurants. It is made from olive oil, vinegar, garlic, fine white bread crumbs, and finely chopped onion, tomato, and cucumber, all well chilled. *Gazpacho* originated as a peasant soup, a sort of "floating salad," but now, in individual bowls set in cracked ice, it has found its way into the most elegant homes and restaurants of Spain.

A seacoast specialty, surprisingly flavorful, is *calamares in su tinta,* or squid in its own juice. The tender pink tentacles of octopus are cooked in the dark liquid contained in a specific portion of the fish, the gravy is thickened, and the whole served with chunks of crisp bread. The sauce is as black as thick ink but the taste is excellent.

Potato omelette is a favorite first course for a family Sunday dinner. An adept cook can flip a dozen small individual omelettes to be arranged on a serving platter, or there may be one large omelette cut into slices like a pie. A slice of this omelette makes an excellent lunch for a farmer or shepherd who must take a noonday meal to the fields on Monday.

Originating in Madrid, and now called by Spaniards "our national dinner," is a long-cooking chickpea stew, called a *cocida*. With the peas are cooked a piece of mutton, a small chicken, spiced sausages, and green vegetables. Often marrow bones are added to give richness and thicken the stew. Frequently the broth is served as a first course, with the meat and vegetables to follow.

Rice *à la Valenciana*, or *paella*, is a superb dish with a rice base. In the rice are cooked a variety of things (as many as the budget can afford), such as chicken, pork, rabbit, peas, artichoke hearts, shrimp, lobster, and crayfish. The entire dish is carefully flavored with garlic and yellow saffron. In the last moments of cooking, small, well-rinsed clams in their shells are inserted, spine-down, in the rice. When the clams steam open, the *paella* is ready to serve.

From northern Asturias comes a hearty version of pork and beans, with Spanish variations. It is called *fabada* (from the word *feba*, or bean) and is made with white beans, a piece of pig's hock, corned beef, salt pork, and onions simmered into tenderness.

Many Basque dishes have a base of salted cod, and from Catalonia come such specialties as stewed partridges and roasted turkey and quail. Often the small game birds are browned and then steamed to completion on a bed of spiced cabbage.

44

This shepherd spends his days tending a small flock of sheep on La Mancha, the vast level plain in the central southwest of Spain. Here the land lies so flat that the sky above also seems flattened, giving an endlessness to the horizon. These sheep are probably driven out to pasture in the early dawn, from a lonely farm or a village barn, and returned at night. In areas where pasturage is scarce, a shepherd may roam with his flocks for miles in a day. Mountain shepherds may stay afield for several days. In winter, when the driving rains are cold, one often sees a shepherd huddled stoop-shouldered under a heavy wool blanket, patiently waiting out the miserable hours as the sheep graze. There is no profit in thin sheep.

Although fresh fruit is by far the most popular dessert with Spaniards, their sweets are important to mention. They seem to specialize in the small sweets, such as sugared almonds and marzipans, nut and honey pastes, shortbreads, honey fritters, and an unusual treat made from candied egg yolk, a specialty of Seville.

The type of food cooked, and the quantity, usually depends on the family budget, but I was most impressed by the excellent food that Spanish housewives with low incomes were able to produce—and hospitably share with me. The *frito misto* platters of a variety of fried fishes, served with big slices of lemon, were very good. Soups, made

45

with a base of a little olive oil instead of meat, were thick, tasty—and original. Often, such a soup might have a dozen artichoke hearts, freshly picked from the garden, a handful of chick peas, shredded cabbage, onions, and perhaps some clams or shrimp from the local fish vendor, all simmered together, and colored lightly with yellow saffron.

Good olive oil, carefully used, gives taste but not *grease* to food. Instead of the bread and peanut butter that American children are given after school, many young Spaniards munch on a piece of bread moistened with olive oil and sprinkled with sugar, between meals.

Spanish dining hours are much different from those in the United States. An average family breakfasts at about eight-thirty on *café con leche* (coffee and hot milk, half and half) and bread and marmalade, as the standard breakfast menu, with the coffee omitted and olive oil substituted for marmalade in poorer homes. Luncheon is the main meal of the day and it is served between two and three in the afternoon. Recently I dined with wealthy friends in Madrid, and our first luncheon course was eggs poached in tomato sauce and served on toast, then came a small green salad, then *filets* of steak wrapped with bacon and broiled, sliced carrots, potato balls, and, for dessert, chocolate mousse with whipped cream, and black coffee. Dinner, served in most Spanish homes between nine and eleven in the evening, is a lighter meal—soups, egg dishes, cold meats, and salads. When they can afford it, Spaniards like to eat very well. Too many, however, cannot afford to eat even enough for minimal health.

In getting an honest picture of present-day Spain, the white-clothed, amply-supplied dinner table must be balanced off by the frequent sight, in small villages or at remote cottages, of a housewife bringing her little iron stove, fueled with charcoal or twigs, out into the street to light. Without a proper indoor kitchen, the smoke and the thin, oily fumes of second-grade olive oil (used both for cooking and as a fire-starter) are shared with the village. Once the fire is properly glowing, the meager meal may be simmered indoors—it is small and simple enough to cook in one pot.

Since food shopping is usually done by the day, most large cities have numbers of neighborhood markets, a series of roofed, open-front

The exquisite and fabled Alhambra is a hillside palace, built outside the southern city of Granada in the thirteenth century when Moorish domination of Spain was at its height. Moroccan in every detail of its design and architecture, the Alhambra was the last major stronghold held by the Moors as they retreated toward the Mediterranean and finally set sail again for Africa, after more than seven hundred years of invasion and occupation. The arches, intricate carvings, and mosaic walls shown here are repeated in variation throughout the vast palace. The tinkle of fountains sounds through every chamber, as does the singing of breezes through arched windows, placed to frame some choice view of orange groves, rocky slopes, or the tumbling Darro River outside. The awkward, rough brick shown behind the Alhambra courtyard in this picture was added long after the completion of the original palace. Its lumpish architecture only seems to accentuate the balance and grace of the Alhambra.

stalls, each selling a specialty such as fruit, vegetables, meat, or fish. In smaller villages, one large market will serve a whole community. The colors and fragrances of fresh food make a pleasant, prosperous perfume and most maids or housewives think of the marketing chores of the day as social occasions.

Spain is just beginning to experiment with frozen foods ("our women are just not that lazy," one Spanish gentleman told me gravely), and there are only a few *supermercados,* or supermarkets—as Americans know them, where all food shopping may be done under one roof. However, the *supermercado,* an establishment named Pryca which recently opened in Madrid, has caused so much approving attention that each day it is as crowded with a combination of shoppers and spectators as a visiting carnival.

Very large and modern, this supermarket is air-conditioned, blares out loud music over the shoppers, has shopping carts, cash registers—everything American supermarkets boast, plus some extra Spanish touches. Canned goods, from Spain, the United States, and northern Europe are plentiful but very expensive. The meat section has conventional meats like beef and lamb, partridges, still in their feathers, wild venison, and economy bargains such as scrawny yellow chicken feet at five cents a pound. The fresh-fish counters are colorful with tiny pink shrimp, great gray-pink tangles of octopus, and huge rounds of fresh tuna. A part of the supermarket is devoted to stalls that sell TV sets, children's underthings, pots and pans, and great bouquets of artificial flowers made in Japan. The mood of the market is gay, raucous, and experimental. Outside, several chauffeur-driven cars are usually parked. Inside, numbers of city-elegant matrons shop through the aisles, followed by uniformed maids pushing shopping carts. At the rear of the market there is a long coffee bar, which sells small cakes, tiny cups of very black coffee and wine, sherry, cognac, and anise by the glass. The supermarket, Pryca, has become the chic, in-town place to have a pre-luncheon drink. Many Madrid businessmen meet their wives there at one o'clock, do a bit of experimental shopping together, have an *apéritif* and wander on home to lunch.

This elaborate cave house is one of many cut into the mountains in the province of Guadalajara, a Moorish word meaning "valley of stones." These cave houses are fairly common in various parts of the country, although few are as elaborate as the two-story, balconied home in the picture. I have seen quite a few just one story high, with a single door to provide both entrance and light, and a short chimney stack protruding from the rock "roof." Many such houses are painted with a broad strip of white or pale blue around the doorway (it would seem presumptuous to whitewash a whole mountain) and are made gay with flower boxes out front. Some are even wired for electricity. Besides offering lower-cost housing, the tenants say these cave buildings can be made snug in winter, while they stay cool even in the blaze of summer.

I noticed one warmly amusing sight at Pryca. Four Spanish workmen, dressed in the dark blue overalls of street cleaners, were checking out their purchases at a cash register: a few slices of sausage, a bit of cheese, a jar of green olives, two long loaves of bread, and a bottle of wine. Almost boyish in their excitement, they then went outside the market to settle on a curbstone under the shade of old chestnut trees, to have lunch.

In spite of wide economic differences, almost all Spaniards are gifted in finding something to give them pleasure.

49

7

Spanish Dancing...Spanish Art

The dances of Spain are like a series of brilliant threads woven into the fabric of the country; a constant activity, in one sense, but varying from region to region, sparkling brightly in the shifting illumination of differing climates, areas and traditions. In the south, Andalusia, there is the famed Flamenco, danced by women in long swirling skirts of red and green and men in high-waisted trousers and flat crowned hats, their heels pounding out a pulsing stacatto beat on floor or table tops, accentuated by the click of castenets. In Pamplona, far to the north, the men always dance along during the fiesta of San Fermin, skipping and weaving through the streets in long snake-lines, accompanied by the music of wandering string bands. In Aragon, there is the graceful, distinctive *Jota* and in Galicia there is regional group dancing, done to the skirl of bagpipes. In Catalonia, the *Sardana* is characteristic, while the brisk *Isa* is typical of the Canary Islands. Special native costumes, often dating back to the local fashions of several centuries ago, are always on hand for special dance *fiestas*.

Dancing in Spain is spontaneous and joyous. At village baptismals and home wedding celebrations, groups gather in the public streets to dance and celebrate. But the dances are rarely whimsical or formless. Whatever the region, the steps follow in the patterns of centuries-old traditions; and to those who perform them with gaiety and brilliance are accorded the respect and homage that would be given to any skilled interpreter of the arts.

Like dancing, art is an integral part of the culture and pleasure of Spain—of its history, too. El Greco and Velasquez are outstanding among the many Spanish artists who have won national and international distinction over the centuries.

Spanish workers leave the fields to dance to the beat of a drum as the wagons roll by.

El Greco—Spanish for "the Greek"—was born on the island of Crete in the mid-sixteenth century, but his soul must always have longed for the gay and somber contradictions of Spain, for there is no Spanish painter who captures this essence more brilliantly and accurately than the man who signed himself "El Greco." He came to Spain, via Italy, as a young man—and typical of painters of his time—began his search for a patron who might support his career. He found a mighty one, Philip II, who was so captivated by El Greco's majestic painting, "The Stripping of Christ Before the Crucifixion" that he commissioned him him to do an altarpiece for El Escorial, the huge monastery-mausoleum which the King was having constructed at that time.

51

Contrary to the fate of many "struggling" painters, El Greco received fame and honor and wealth within his lifetime (1541-1614). His work is instantly identifiable in museums and churches throughout Spain (and the world): tall, attenuated figures, in somber colors, with faces haunted by visions of the world of the spiritual soul. Domenicus Theotocopoulous, El Greco, is—in a sense—the most Spanish of painters, in all his work there is the brown earth and brown leathers of Spain, the tawny lights of sun filtered through olive trees, and all the glorious

In his self-portrait, El Greco pictures himself as St. Luke, his patron. The painting is in the Cathedral of Toledo, Spain.

The Crucifixion, *painted by El Greco.*

contradictions of the country he chose to celebrate with his genius.

The name of Diego Rodriguez de Silva y Velasquez also shines out amidst the giants of Spanish art. Born in 1599, the son of prosperous parents (his father was a lawyer in Seville), Velasquez set out early to master the techniques of painting. With rigid discipline, he concentrated first on deceptively simple things: still-lifes of fish, fruit and water jugs. But such studies did not long satisfy his vaulting imagination.

The aim of his artistic purpose was two-fold: a photographic accuracy to his subjects, for one, and, secondly, by close study, as well as by color and physical detail, to catch the spirit, mood and personality of each individual he painted. (He once did more than a thousand sketches of the same model, a young man who served him as a companion-valet, in an attempt to trap all the transitory expressions on his

The Maids of Honour, *painted by Don Diego Rodriguez de Silva Y Velazquez in 1656, which originally hung in the old Royal Palace, the Alcazar at Madrid, is now in the Prado Museum, Madrid. The central figure is the Infanta Margarita who has come to the studio of Velazquez to see the portrait of her parents (reflected in the mirror in the background). She is attended by her two maids of honour and two dwarfs. The artist has painted himself, standing at his easel to the left.*

The great Spanish painter, Velazquez, produced this spirited equestrian portrait of Prince Balthasar Carlos, youngest son of Philip IV, who was a lifelong patron of the artist. This may be seen in the Prado Museum, Madrid.

face). Velasquez married young, had two children, and came to Madrid to live at the age of twenty-five.

His mature paintings reflect the breadth of his own brilliant imagination: they range from studies of mythology and Christianity, to those on which his fame is most securely founded—the magnificent portraits of the personages of the Court of King Philip. These are history as well as great art; biographies on canvas. They give us forever the flavor of the period, faithfully and radiantly mirroring its splendors and its ugliness—in short, its humanity.

8

Thank You...I Speak English

Of course, the majority of Spaniards do not speak English, or any language other than their mother tongue, but an impressive number of well-educated Spaniards are able to converse in Spanish, English, French, and perhaps a little German. In that country, sharply divided into economic classes, where higher education is still for the few, to be a student is a serious, important responsibility. Thus an educated Spaniard is often very well educated indeed.

Education in Spain ranges from the very old to the very new. The world-renowned University of Salamanca dates from the thirteenth century and in the sixteenth century, more than 7,000 students were enrolled there. Christopher Columbus consulted with the University's professors of astronomy before setting out on his historic sail for the Americas. The "new" are the numbers of simple, small elementary schools that have been built over the face of Spain, starting at the end of the Civil War in 1939, and continuing—at the pace of a fast snail—until today.

By law, Spanish children are required to go to school from the age of six to twelve, either in one of the 75,000 state schools or one of the 25,000 private schools. In the larger cities and towns, most children trot off to school with promptness and regularity, taking a two-hour break at midday to go home for luncheon with the entire family. But in impoverished or remote areas, where people are too poor to provide school clothes for large families or where a school simply does not exist, scores of children never get much reading-and-writing education.

After twelve, those young Spaniards who do not go on to school may simply begin to work with their fathers or relatives, on farms and in vineyards or on fishing boats, while the girls can always give their

This neat peak-roofed house and barn combination is typical of dwellings in the rich farm land outside Valencia, although red-tiled roofs, with a lesser pitch, are equally common. The whitewash of the two fruit trees and the small bread oven in front of the house not only give the homestead a trim look but indicate prideful ownership: "If it's mine, I'll paint it." Such houses are usually sparsely furnished: an eating table, some cane-bottomed chairs, metal cots for sleeping, a sewing machine, and a few religious pictures on the walls. Laundry will be done in a community washhouse nearby. One thing this picture cannot show: the sound of a radio blaring out music over the countryside. In rural Spain, the rule seems to be, the smaller the house, the louder the radio.

mothers a hand with housework or younger children. Many boys work for a number of years as apprentices, at small pay, to learn to be mechanics, metalworkers, construction helpers, or other skilled manual trades. Currently, about 10,000 young student-workers are pupils at six "labor high schools," scattered throughout Spain, where students receive two years of routine elementary education and then up to seven years of training in special subjects such as agriculture, metallurgy, electricity, textiles, and the technology of foodstuffs.

According to figures given out by the Spanish Government, there are currently about 4,000,000 children in the country's elementary schools, with a secondary-school population of about 500,000. That means that only one out of eight young Spaniards currently continues his education into the high-school years and considerably fewer go beyond.

However, there are thirteen old and established Spanish universities where a student may get degrees in any of the major branches of learning—Medicine, Science, Philosophy, Letters, and so on. There are now about 68,000 students in these universities, and at the modern, sprawling University of Madrid (much of this campus has been built since the end of the Spanish Civil War) there are today 29,000 undergraduates.

Spaniards, on the whole, are an usually alert, responsive people (this is the nation that produced Cervantes, Goya, Velázquez, Cortes, Magellan, and hundreds of great names that ring through the entire world history of arts, letters, and human achievement), so we cannot measure their "education" simply by the numbers of years spent in classrooms. Among the special pleasures of Spain are the general high level of intelligence and the artistic curiosity of the people.

Spaniards are great traditionalists and their social and religious life is hung together by a series of holidays, *fiestas*, and *ferias* that string through the calendar like a series of bright pearls. Many are centuries old in custom.

Of all the religious holidays, aside from Christmas the most important is *Semana Santa*, the Holy Week ceremonies preceding Easter Sunday. Every town and village has its own religious processions, but Seville and Malaga are most famous for their splendid, glittering, candlelit, flower-scented parades, with the various statues of the Blessed Virgin carried through the streets each night for a week.

In Valencia, the *Fallas of San José*—held during the week in March in which Saint Joseph's name day falls—are as hectic and exuberant as *Semana Santa* is sobering and subdued. There are parades, fireworks, dances, and at-home parties. Then, on the last night of the *fiesta*, all the *fallas* (great groups of statues made of cardboard, wax, and bright paint) are burned in the town squares.

Spanish futbol, *or soccer, is a sport so popular that it can fill Madrid's two major stadiums every Sunday afternoon during the playing season. Most smaller towns also have stadiums, and games between town teams can create as much tension and rivalry as any baseball game in the World Series of the United States. Urban newsstands carry sports fan magazines patterned after American movie magazines. Many city teenagers feel that* futbol *is a more modern and hence a more "in" sport than the traditional Spanish bullfight. In the fields beyond the Stadium Santiago Bernabeu, shown in this picture, are the shells of several modern apartment buildings under construction. In the rapid buildup of Madrid's housing program, not only are those buildings now completed, they are already tightly surrounded by blocks and blocks of neighbors.*

The elaborate spring *feria* of Seville, with music, dancers, and bull-fights, is the "queen fair" of all Spain, but some time during the summer months every little village has its fair, with game booths, dancing, candies for the children—and a general air of festivity and relaxation throughout the whole village.

These special holidays might be listed by the hundreds, but it is their character, not their names, that is important. They affect Spanish life for everyone. Whole towns turn out for the fun—or the reverence—depending on the mood of the celebration. There are few stay-at-homes among the extrovert Spaniards.

On bright Sunday afternoons, bull rings and soccer stadiums alike are jammed with crowds. In the north, tournament *pelota* is popular, pigeon shoots are frequent, and Basque villages are famous for their woodcutting contests. (Two men, two axes, and two equally thick logs—which will split his tree the faster?) Movies have long been popular in Spain and many, both Spanish and foreign, are now produced in several large studios in Madrid. The generally clear weather and good light for photographing, plus the availability of skilled technicians at reasonable wages, has made Spain the third largest motion-picture-producing country in the world, after the United States (Hollywood) and Japan. In large cities, movie seats are reserved in advance and often on Sundays, Spanish urbanites will pick up tickets for an evening show on the way home from Mass. In the villages, movie houses are usually simple affairs, with folding chairs for seats, and the whole town jamming in around ten o'clock at night—for the first showing. Although first-rate movies are frequently shown in the larger towns, the village movie houses seem to get films about as fresh as those run on the late-late TV shows in the United States. "Tough" Jimmy Cagney, "romantic" Randolph Scott, and a "young" Rita Hayworth are still very active on rural Spanish screens.

Television has come to Spain only in a half dozen of the larger cities. There are excellent evening news broadcasts, a few live variety shows —plus popular American series, such as *The Nurses, Ben Casey, The Dick Powell Show*, and many others.

Yet, for all the outside entertainment available and enjoyed, Spain is still a "family nation" and probably the single most popular form of recreation is the *paseo*, which, in translation, means simply "walk." Spaniards are obviously the greatest pleasure walkers in the world. The *paseo* is a social affair, a promenade for exercise, chatting, and greeting friends. *Novios* and *novias* or whole families like to take a leisurely stroll up a boulevard or village street, or through the park. On Sunday afternoons or before the evening dinner hour, the *paseo* is a time for parents to show off their children, or for a young man to be proud of his fiancée—no one goes on a *paseo* without being carefully groomed. On holidays, whole towns come alive with citizens out taking the air,

Seed corn drying on a wooden balcony, sunlight tuck pointing worn stones, a woman stooping to fill a clay jug at the village fountain: this rocky little crossroads scene was photographed in a small village near historic Cáceres, in the western province of Estremadura. "If these old stones could talk," as the cliché goes, they might tell of the sprawling Roman camp established nearby in the year seventy-four, of the four separate and fierce battles waged by the Spanish to reclaim this area from the Moors, and of the great explorers, Cortes, De Soto, and Pizarro, all of whom came from this province, hugging along the Portuguese border. Although part of the countryside is devoted to pasture land and farming, Estremadura still has deep stretches of wooded land, rugged hills fragrant with wild asters and peonies, and eagles nesting in loneliness. Near the villages, orchards thrive and sheep graze the hills. Acorn-fed pigs, from which come distinctively good ham and sausage, are typical of Estremadura.

This old arched Roman bridge over the Guadaira River in the province of Seville is still used to carry grapes by truck or donkey cart to the winery on the riverbank. Spain's southern rivers, often slow trickles or even beds of dry stones in the summer months, make superb picnic spots. As shown here, an olive grove meandering down to the water gives cooling shade, the little cluster of whitewashed buildings at the foot of the bridge probably has a bodega *to sell bread, cheese, and wine— plus a few salty green olives sold in a cone of brown paper. One of the special treats of Spain is to be found in its peaceful, rural silences.*

to watch and be watched. Sidewalk cafés are filled with the pleasant chatter of a half-hour spent with a glass of sherry—and friends.

The energetic personality, the *caballero,* or the "gentleman" standard which each Spaniard sets for himself makes Spain an excellent country to visit. Almost overrich in history, tradition, art treasures, and breathtaking scenery, the Spaniard seems ever eager to share the pleasures of his birthplace.

When a Spanish man or woman is introduced to a stranger, the customary greeting is a simple and graceful word: *"Encantada"*—"I am delighted."

Somehow, in Spain, one never doubts the sincerity of that expression.

Index

MAUREEN DALY

was born in County Tyrone, Northern Ireland, and grew up in Fon du Lac, Wisconsin. She first won literary distinction when she was fifteen, with a short story entitled *Fifteen*, which placed fourth in a national short story contest sponsored by *Scholastic Magazine*. The next year she won first place with a story called *Sixteen*, which was selected for the annual O. Henry Memorial Award volume. Her first novel, *Seventeenth Summer*, won the *Dodd, Mead Intercollegiate Literary Fellowship* contest and quickly became a best seller. She has never stopped writing since—writing vigorously, simply, and always with a new appeal.

Her articles and short stories have appeared in many national magazines, and, as a report-columnist for the *Chicago Tribune*, and, later, as associate editor of *Ladies Home Journal* and consultant to the editors of the *Saturday Evening Post*, Miss Daly toured the United States, writing about and observing the American scene. In 1952, Miss Daly was awarded the American Freedom Foundation Medal for reporting. *Mention My Name in Mombasa*, written with her husband, William P. McGivern, and her *Spanish Roundabout* are fresh, spirited reports of visits to Europe and Africa.

Seventeenth Summer is currently in preparation for movie production by Warner Brothers, and *The Ginger Horse* will be seen as a Walt Disney television presentation.